LEAD
Get Up & Ignite the Hustle

Dr. Wilson L. Triviño

Aura Free Press

Copyright © 2015 by Dr. Wilson Lubin Triviño

All rights reserved. No part of this book may be used or reproduced in any manner whatsoever without prior written consent of the author, except as provided by the United States of American copyright law.

Published by Aura Free Press, Marietta, Georgia USA

ISBN-10: 0-9743226-5-2
ISBN-13: 978-0-9743226-5-0

Dedication

To my nieces: Gabriella and Arianna Triviño, that they may continue their Tiós Wilson and David's hustle. That they not forget the sacrifices of their abuelitos from Colombia, S.A., Lubin and Aura Triviño, who left everything from the old world so their family could live their dreams in the new one. At 9 and 6 years old these young women are living messengers to a world that I will never see. I love you both.

Also by Dr. Wilson L. Triviño

Organizational Change Within the Social Security Administration: An Assessment of the National Partnership for Reinvention Policy in the Southern Region (2002) (2015)

Remember Your ABCs: A Simple Guide on how to become a success and life the life YOU want to lead! (2003)

Remember Your ABCs Lite: Quotes and ideas that will empower you to live the life YOU want to lead! (2003) (with C. David Triviño, Esq.)

ABCs of Live Streaming: Harness the Power of Social Media (2015)

ABC Vision: A simple guide on the ABCs of Success and how to live the life you want to lead! (2015)

Love, Love, Love (2015)

Table of Contents

Dedication iii

Also by Dr. Wilson L. Triviño iv

Acknowledgements vii

Prologue 9

Chapter 1 Let's do this 11

Chapter 2 Leadership 17

Chapter 3 Entrepreneurship 27

Chapter 4 Action 39

Chapter 5 Dream Big 49

Chapter 6 Get Up & Ignite the Hustle 53

References 57

About the Author 62

"Your memories must not over shadow your dreams, your dreams are your aspirations of the future."
Dr. Betty Siegel

Acknowledgements

I want to thank my parents: Lubin and Aura Triviño and all that have contributed to my success.

Especially my lawyer, brother, and best friend, C. David Triviño, Esq. who always sees the best in people in this chaotic world. He reminds me every day that our best days are ahead of us. The people's lawyer that never backs down from doing the right thing. A fighter for justice. Follow him @T4Vista. Hire him for legal representation.

I am also grateful to be part of the American odyssey and hope to do my part to "make America Great again". It is more than hope and change, but action in 2016.

> "Things do not happen.
> Things are made to happen."
> John F. Kennedy

Prologue

"Don't look for love, live it!"
Leo Buscaglia

Hello Friend-

I hear the roar of thunder outside. I feel the tremble. At these moments I embrace the power of mother nature. I feel so small in comparison to the world around me. I am but a speck. But it is not the size of the dog in the fight, but the size of the fight in the dog. Life is a struggle, a fight, a series of ups and downs. I do love kitty cats and know we need more purrs and less of a hiss in today's world.

We live in a era of uncertainty. 2015 has been a challenge with all the violence and continued economic turmoil. I want this book to be a proactive step to collectively change our mindset. To end the year on a high note. To begin a clean slate in 2016.

I want to thank you for picking up this book. I hope that these ideas will empower you to live your dreams. If you don't agree then pass it along to someone else. My hope is that these writings will ignite your hustle. That you will "get up" from your troubles and live your dreams. All we have is this moment. The past is gone, the future is not guaranteed, we just have this moment of time. Time stops for no man.

If you see me in real life (IRL), say 'hello', let's share a moment an ideas.

Follow me on social media @abcvision for all my writings on reviews, ideas, and positive quotes. Do send me a shout out!

Together we will blaze a path. Create a new world full of hope and love. Opportunities are everywhere. All you have to do is create the best one for you. Stay fabulous.

I love you,

Dr. Wilson L. Triviño
Innovation Center - @abcvision
Atlanta, Georgia USA
December 25, 2015

Dr. Wilson Lubin Triviño @abcvision

"Keep your face to the sunshine and you cannot see a shadow."
Helen Keller

Chapter 1 Let's do this

"Change your thoughts, change your world."
Dr. Wilson Triviño

Hello friend. It is 3 am, I can't sleep and I am sipping tea. I turn to the news on my iPhone and it is over flowing with soundbites about the global war on terror. Reactions from American politicians who want to build a wall to keep the "bad guys out." A big wall, a humane wall. Come on now, like we really can block out all the evil doers. It did not work for the Chinese in their great wall centuries ago, how will it work for the USA? We need to embrace the flow of people and ideas. To be part of the global village. I turn off the social media noise and my achey body tells me it wants to stay in bed. It wants to just stay there in a resting state as the world. To lie dormant and shut off the world around me. To just be. But I feel a force inside me. This book is ready to come out. Here we go.

At 45 years old, I don't know if I have passed that half way mark of my life, but I still yearn to leave a mark, blaze a path in my life's journey. I have reached many of my big goals but still have more to go on to. Should I just lay here and listen to doubt or feel the spirit that says, "get up". That inner voice we all have, the one that tells us what is right from wrong. The one that comes from our inner soul, touches our gut and leads us on the right path.

In the quiet of the night, it is loud and direct. It stays with me throughout the day, but now it is clear. To shed some light in the world full of darkness. But focus on a world that is full of hope and joy.

As I write this, *Creed* (2015), the movie is out. It continues the saga of Rocky, but this time Rocky is the coach. Rocky (Sylvester Stallone) is an all too familiar face, we have seen him rise and fall. How he is appropriate pop culture character in our fast pace world. He now is mentor to "Creed" the young fighter who is hungry to make his mark, to be a champion. Rocky's most important piece of advice is shared in a candid scene with his mentee. As the young man practices his punches in the small gym in front of a mirror, Rocky tells him to look hard at the reflection, for that is the toughest opponent. In this movie, he is the one that you must beat the man in the mirror. That is so true. Our worst critic lies inside of us. The little voice, the third roommate in our head. The one pointing out our flaws, the mistakes, and our weaknesses. The one that punches us in the gut, even when we are down. Rocky is from the old school, focused on the fundamentals, a local boy from Philly to just "get up" and fight.

This book is about the focus. About the importance of needing to "get up" every day. Even after we have been knocked down. Life is hard and is full of atrocities. Today our society is conditioned to be scared. To fear the unknown, unknown. We can't allow the terrorist to fuel our fear. We must stand up and face the risks. You can't be insulated in a perfect cocoon. The only place you could do that was inside your mother's womb. There, for nine months you had everything, but suddenly were ejected, you were on your own, broken from the direct link to your mama's love. Cold, wet, and hungry and things get worse.

You need to spark a fire within you to enjoy the good things in this world. To condition yourself to look at the "bright side of life". Don't be a polyanna but take charge of your thoughts. That is the real power you have.

We live in a hyper connected community, we know in an instance what is going on in the farthest reaches of the planet, but sometimes it is that internal dialogue where we are clueless. We don't listen to our instincts, learn from our mistakes, and take the risks to grab that golden ring.

We hear political slogans like "make America great again" and it more than simply beating up on the weak. It should mean that we are going to create a blazing path to a better future. To shift the paradigm. Empower the mind and be free to live our own life's story. To be a success and live the life we want to lead. We yearn for the good old days but they were not that good. The best days do lie in front of us. We just need to remind ourselves of that. We need to be winners, not be satisfied with the status quo.

What makes the United States an exceptional place is that we have the freedom to control our thoughts and ideas. To take advantage of the world around us. That exceptionalism is what has kept us on top. To have a system built on opportunities for all. We the people. It is up to us, no one else. We need to wake up, the blame game needs to stop. If it is going to be, it's up to me. It is upon us to create a path to success. This book counters all the negative noise I hear from our news media, political leaders, and pop culture. To remind each of us that we will break through the funk and be "great again."

This book title, *LEAD- Get Up & Ignite the Hustle* is a framework to get you started. A framework to start moving forward. To open your world to possibility instead of building walls of isolation. Each letter is a trigger to a focus.

L- Leadership
E- Entrepreneurship
A-Action
D-Dream big

L is for leadership. Those that want to move forward must get out front. Become a leader and build a team of success. E is for entrepreneurship. Entrepreneurs are innovative and implement an action plan. They don't see obstacles but opportunities. A is for action. To take steps to make a difference. I share my template of success, the ABCs, all about your Attitude, Beliefs, and Commitment. Finally and the most important is to Dream Big. To take this world full of adventure and make it your own. How do you do that? You take time to develop a mission and capture your inner passion.

Life is not one big or small moment, it is a series of passages. Of highs and lows that allow us to project the story of our lives on the big screen. To create our narrative and be happy. To always have something to look forward to. Ted Kennedy shared in his book *Compass* that life is really can be captured in a cycle of three major turns. One, to have something to look forward to. A party, a celebration, an accomplishment or something of significance. Two, to experience the moment. To enjoy the toast of champagne, that first fizzle of bubbly. A great meal, a show, family time, the joy of a kitten purring as you rub their soft fur. You get the idea. Something warm and fuzzy. Third, to have a great memory of it. To remember those who love you, that fantastic meal, that beautiful sunrise. I could expand a hundred fold, but you get the gist. The continuous cycle of life. It has a beginning, a middle, and an end. But the journey is what makes a life worth living. To have ambitious goals and dreams. To take charge and live your life. We allow ourselves to be flooded with information and drown from the inability to act. Make this your day. LEAD!

I saw a post on Instagram that had this 80s dressed looking fellow holding and wearing twenty gadgets. From a video camera, Walkman, camera, telephone, etc and the caption read "now we carry all these in our front pocket". I thought to myself, "wow", yes how my world has changed since the 80s, but that voice inside my head is still the same. It is wiser and more cautious but it is still telling me what I should do. My gut feeling on what is right and wrong. We don't listen to that voice, we allow the external noise cloud our judgement.

No matter what is going on with you, I want you to "get up" and ignite the hustler. You don't have to be a fast talking smooth brother but I am referring to your dreams. To that list you have of all the things you want to do while you are on this journey. What's your bucket list. Things to do be before you die. Nothing if forever. No matter how big or small, it can be done. What happens is we settle and give up. I want this book to be your wake up call. Dynamite comes in small packages and this book is ready to pop! Boom, Boom, pow!

LEAD- Get up & ignite the hustle.

Dr. Wilson Lubin Triviño @abcvision

"Conflict cannot survive without your participation."
Wayne W. Dyer

Chapter 2 Leadership

"You can get anything you want as long as you help other people get anything they want."
Zig Ziglar

Some may wonder why I start off with a chapter on leadership. Life's adventures is not the end it all but only a means to get what you want. That is why in my writings focus on you as an individual and discover the concise message you want to broadcast. Leadership is easy, it is hard take steps to become one. To stand out front and be the one that says, "let's go this way." You need to show up, stand up, and stand out.

Leadership is something that is often mentioned but poorly taught. I have spent my life time studying leadership. Coming from an immigrant family, I have seen firsthand the willingness to be innovative, to carve out a new path and to strive for success. I have met every US President since Gerald Ford, heard every top speaker in every genre in the lasts twenty five years and read thousands of books. I have concluded there is no clear path to becoming a leader. But one thing is for sure, you can foster the leader from within and become one.

To be a leader at anything, you got to do what it takes. In today's multidimensional world, talent does not cut it. More people are competing for your job. The kids of today have to worry about the child in China and India, not simply like I did, only worry about Pee Wee down the street.

Just to be clear. It is ok, if you don't want to be a leader and just a follower. That is fine. But I want to focus my writings in this book to those who want to become a leader. The ones that want to start living the life they want to lead. To say, I am not going to take it anymore, I am taking charge of my destiny. If you don't buy this message then pass this book along to someone that will. The person that is willing to do what it takes to start taking charge and plot their future.

Are leaders made or simply born that way? I think it is a combination of education, experience, and internal drive. I am a first born and have always been an alpha male. This rank has many blessings and pressures. You are the first to do anything and also the first to your newly minted parents. You are in essence the test case. I blazed the path for my 3 brothers to follow.

There are many categories of leadership: the charismatic leader, the emotional intelligent leader, the servant leader, the dictator leader. There even is a method of holacracy that proclaims to run an organization with no central leader. Zappos the show company under Tony Hsieh is implementing holacracy. But in today's world where technology has forced the focus to the individual, so much of success is to be driven and self-directed. Ideas are the most valuable currency in the information age. But how do you break out from the noise and carve a path? Virgin CEO Sir Richard Branson shares his take on leadership with the three Ls: to listen, learn, and laugh. At a Captain Planet event in Atlanta, Branson jumped on stage and lifted his host in a boyish manner. He was such full of life, but seemed to be a boy having fun and it did lighten up this stuffy crowd.

I believe in you, more importantly believe in yourself. I want this book to be a wakeup call. To discover or re-discover your passion and use the tools of the digital age to plug in and pull up toward your dreams. All the answers lie within but sometimes we need a kick in the pants to wake up and say "yes we can!"

My strategy for leadership are these tenets:

1- Do it!
2- Vision
3- Dream team
4- Decide
5- Change

Do it!

Talk is cheap. You can read and study leadership, but until you have taken a leadership role you do not know what type of leader you can become. Take this opportunity to become a leader.

If you are already a leader then work on becoming a better one. Listen, learn, and lead, we all have access to all the information that has ever existed in the palms of our hands, take charge and lead.

In today's world, there is no longer a corporate gentlemen's agreement that if you work for one company, you will be taken care of when you retire. According to the bureau of labor statistics the average worker currently holds ten different jobs before the age of 40. Forrester Research projects that today's millennial will hold twelve to fifteen jobs in their lifetime. This means that you must take charge. Be your own CEO and become a leader. It's not an option to sit and wait to be recognized. You must take action. You must awaken the leader from within. To be in control within organization.

Stand up and I guarantee people will follow. Most don't have the guts to stand up, they simply whine and complain. Blend into the cogs of the organization and muddle throughout their career. Sometimes you have to grab life by the balls. In the South we have PBR, no I don't mean that beer by that name, but professional bull riding. How do those little guys hop on those bulls and command them? They have a strap that squeezes the bull's boys and off they go. It is not hard to be a leader, you just got to be one. To step up and take charge.

Vision

Leaders have a vision and share it. Faith and determination can help you move mountains but sometimes you need to realize that all you need to do is move around it.

Having goals, planning a strategy are important. Muddling through a situation is never the best way to achieve desired results. Being proactive in today's world is the key to find these hidden gems of opportunity.

We are all born with dreams. Go to a classroom of children and they want to be astronauts, presidents, or artist. None say they want to be a junior analyst or an associate at a so so firm. They have big aspirations. What happens over the years is we conform and become complacent. If we do break free, we are often shun or seen as an outcast, part of the freaks and geeks. The frog that jumps into the water on the stove when it is lukewarm does not know the heat is slowly rising and is about get cooked.

Take time and reflect. It is important that we disconnect with the outer world and connect with the inner world. Ask yourself, "What would you do if you had all the time and money in the world? Who would you be? How can you help the greater web of existence?"

Spell it out and write down your goals. List all the things you want to accomplish, then start breaking them down into action plans. One small step starts the path of a long journey.

Leaders rise to the top. They take risk and are not afraid to hang out with other eagles and not congregate with turkeys. Eagles fly and that is where you want to be, flying high above. I am a war eagle. Time and time again I ask folks that are in their 80s and 90s what they would do differently if they had to live their life over. The most common answer is they would have taken more risk. To not be afraid, to realize early on that in life it all works out. The earlier you realize that, the quicker you can get to living your dreams today.

Mark Cuban shares that he is credited with being a risk taker. Not true. He studies the issue. He seeks out areas he is weak. He is not afraid to ask. Often we get embarrassed or are in positions of power and have a false sense we know it all. Entrepreneurs take risks, but they also increase the potential for a bigger prize.

Dream Team

I admit I am a lone wolf, but even I realize I can't do everything myself. I need to work with individuals to help me get closer to my goals. There is no 'I' in team so realize that to climb the tall mountain of success you need to bring resources together. Social media empowers you to reach out to those that are doing it. Don't become them, but borrow the best practice and improve on others success. Social media allows you to tap into your community, your peeps, and your peoples. Like minded individuals that can help.

I think you can learn a lot from super heroes. They have super powers, they always are doing work for the common good, they have a 360 degree view, and they work with other super heroes. What are your super powers? What do you bring to the table? What are your weaknesses? What is your kryptonite? Find those that compliment your weaknesses. George W. Bush said that one lesson he learned being President is that you have all the power, but not all the answers. Often you have to rely on others. Don't be afraid of smarter people around you on your team.

It is important to have a vision, but you need a structure to implement this vision. Organizations exist for a reason. They provide a service, produce a product, or implement a public policy. They exist in many forms and are found in every aspect of human civilization. To achieve an understanding, of their dynamics, one must ask, "What do organizations do and how well do they do it?" Organizations serve a purpose, but they do not exist in a vacuum. In the much larger universe of which they are a part, both internal and external forces exert an influence on them. The literature within the field of organizational theory is vast and wide-ranging. Organizations have a life cycle. We must be aware of the structure around us. The networks, the methods and the processes that we have created to live our lives. Too often in this golden age of civilization we muddle through life rather than take charge and have an action plan.

There is a story of Henry Ford that when he wanted to build the V-8 engine, he was frustrated that it was not coming along. He went to speak to the engineers and they said it was impossible. He immediately fired everyone and hired a new team. Today we have the V-8 engine.

The fly-by of Pluto is another great story. It was the mission that almost never was. It had obstacle over obstacle, but a core group of scientist did the impossible, to take a baby grand piano size device that used little power and to beam pictures back to earth from the outer rim of our galaxy. It only took 15 years to get there.

Decide

Work is called that for a reason, it is work. Whatever your profession is, you have responsibilities. Have timelines and targets to keep track of your progress. The old adage goes, the organization does what the boss check is often the case. But in being able to accomplish big objectives you need to have measurable results. You need to make sure what you are doing is working. The definition of insanity is doing the same thing over and over and expecting a different result. Write down your goals and break them down. Set time tables and follow it. As the Chinese proverb ask, "how do you eat an elephant?" The answer: one bite at a time. So write down your goals and break it down into small bites. Develop a plan, seat of the pants leadership will get you only so far.

Today's world is both a blessing and a curse. We don't have one or two options, we have thousands. This overwhelm overload of information creates indecisiveness. Being a leader is more than being a leader but making a decision. President George W. Bush memoir *Decision Points* is broken down into chapters of major decisions in his life. Not all were political, but they were forks in the road that had an impact. Often I see leaders not make a decision but muddle through. This can be safe for a while until the house of cards comes crashing down.

Be aware of the world around you. Good leaders are able to break from the noise and see what the mega trends are outside to their universe. Don't get stuck in a silo. Reach out to other sectors and be a sponge to ideas.

That is why listening to what those around you are saying is important. Not simply to yes people, but people that are doing what you want to do. Be aware of ideas and borrow them. God gave you two ears and one mouth, use them accordingly. Don't get stuck in a silo. Reach from outside the bubble. You can't be an expert on everything so reach out to build your base so that you will will be a better leader. Don't be afraid to say I don't know.

You want to surround yourself with individuals that are making it. For example if you walk into a room with nine broke people, you will know who the tenth will be. I am not just talking about money, but broke in ideas. Social media has broken down walls, flatten the landscape. Now you can connect with folks you want to emulate. See how they are doing it and replicate their method. You can't be them, but you can replicate the path. Rise up. Be a winner. Grant Cardone is fond of saying, "if you are not first, you are last."

It is more than being connected, but to connect. To use emotional intelligence and really understand your organization and serve those around you. Daniel Goldman research points to the invaluable resource of being able to use emotional intelligence to lead others. The non-verbal cues to understand what is being said.

Part of having a 360 degree view of the world around you is to build relationships. Harvey MacKay in his book *Dig Your Well before You're Thirsty* shares that the average funeral has 200 attendees. That means that at least 200 folks cared enough about the deceased to attend his funeral. In essence we have on an average a network of 200 people around us. So think about every person you meet as having a 200 person network that can help you in your dreams. Social media will expand it. Seek connectors, as Malcolm Gladwell writes about.

I will take it one step forward. In networking, it is more than exchanging your business card or LinkedIn info. You need to connect. Have a common bond and build on it. I believe that is why your approach should be to "net weave". Bob Littell's concept is simple, to weave a bond. Like taking a thread all across a quilt, weave a string across the tapestry. Build a brand and share it with others and they will help you. Using the golden rule and be a connector of others, to engage, empower, and energize.

Carl Sandberg was fond of saying that "if you go to a party you have a moral obligation to be interesting". The second part I add, is a page from Dale Carnegie which is to be interesting is to be "interested".

God gave us two ears and one mouth, so use them proportionally. Listen, learn, and lead should be your battle cry.

What is so powerful with social media is that now you have a channel to plug into with an endless network. The shift from a six degree of separation comes down to the power of one. Anyone you want to meet or connect is one person away. That is power. That is what the modern age has created. But the first step is for you to know what you want.

Use social media not only to tell your story but to show it. Piggy back on trends. Do your research and put the message into the context of the content. Ask questions and engage.

Mark Cuban spoke to the success of business pitches. Know your business, share that vision, and communicate it. As on the television show *Shark Tank*, we all get these defining moments, be ready to jump through the opening and grab the brass ring.

Change

Change is so big in our world today. The pace is accelerating faster and faster, but sometimes we forget that it has always been a part of life. The seasons, the spinning of the earth, the advancement of society. Biologically you have changed since you started reading this book.

Change is much more than the coins in your pocket. It's part of living. One of the fields I study is the literature of organizational change. We are the center of our universe and our organization. One of the greatest opportunities for development as a whole and for its staff as individuals, occurs during times of crisis. Change is inevitable for individuals, organizations, and society. Change is epidemic, but it is frequently unpredictable and uncontrollable and the rate of change appears to be increasing. If this constant state of flux is unsettling for individuals, it is doubly so for organizations. Change is not understood, and there are few recognized ways to cope with it from an organizational perspective. Change disturbs equilibrium and disrupt relationships within an environment. Change comes in many forms, and not all are beneficial – change always involves costs as well as benefits. Even if change is ultimately beneficial, organizations, like individuals, frequently resist and resent it. The inevitable of change and the necessity for organizations to adapt to it make it one of the most important concerns of contemporary organization theory.

Organizations experience shifts over time and may need to change significantly each time. The need to change is the need to grow. Having the ability to adapt constantly to a shifting environment enables organizations to survive. A sprawling literature addresses organizational change and innovation of which much focuses on how to change for the better. Successful organizational change is not easy but the ones that are able to adapt survive.

If you are not green on the vine, then you are dying. So keep a focus on how you can plug in and apply best practices. Ideas matter and there is no better way than to implement something that works rather than try to reinvent the wheel. How do you embrace change and conquer it? Take charge. Don't be the victim, be the innovator.

It is important to listen to that inner voice and your gut instinct. When you feel that pull, your brain is bringing you inner and outer voice to give you direction to innovate.

This strategy is one way to become a leader the go to person. To stand up and have others follow your trailblazing path. Be a leader and if you are one be a better one. We need more eagles and less turkeys. Eagles rise above the fray.

Chapter 3 Entrepreneurship

"You can't have a million dollar dream with a minimum wage work ethic."
Stephen C. Hogan

What does it take to be an entrepreneur? Countless studies, books, and articles have been written. But first you have to have the willingness to hustle and not give up. The hustle never stops and money never sleeps. This line comes from Michael Douglas character in *Wall Street: Money Never Sleeps* but it is applicable to your life's goals today. The **HUSTLE** stands for **H**ow **U** **S**urvive **T**hrough **L**ife **E**veryday! This book's title has the word hustle. Why, because I believe you have to be hungry. To always want to accomplish your dreams. No matter how big or small. To be looking forward to something.

If you want to be an entrepreneur, do it. If you don't then don't. However if you don't start building your dream, someone else will hire you to build their dream. Time is the great equalizer and what success in business equates is freedom. The freedom to do whatever you want. To carve out your path. To have choices.

What makes a good entrepreneur? The old adage is true, you have a good product and ask lots of people to buy.

I have been fortunate to have an entrepreneurship mindset most of my life. This came from my parents. My dad was the visionary, the outside guy and my mother was the inside gal, keeping the books and being the conservative voice. She was the one with the rosary beads worrying, but my father had faith. He took risks.

He came to the USA with $90 and a dream in 1968. He had heard of how the USA streets were paved with gold. How anything was possible. He wanted to provide for his family. Yes, it worked for him, but today many are not seeking that same dream. They are complacent.

My father is a transmission man, cars are his business and have always been a part of my world. I did not inherit his mechanical skill set but did get the entrepreneur gene. My dad is always looking for new money making opportunities and is full of ideas.

I started pumping gas at the shop, making change and dealing with customers at age 7. I have sold all type of products, help organize million dollar projects, and started many different businesses. I am an idea person, but am a naturally born salesman. In our world today, being a salesman has taken on a bad connotation. Kind of like being a lawyer or politician. But being in sales is the cornerstone of any successful business venture. Even in life, you got to sell yourself every day.

Those Dale Carnegie techniques are timeless and we have lost in our society those old school salesmen. I am a graduate of a Dale Carnegie course and can't tell you how many times the techniques and ideas have come in handy. Be it in business or personal affairs.

Bernie Marcus of Home Depot shares in his talks that many folks ask him how he became so successful. He says he only sold to his friends. So his job was to make new "friends". Marcus paid for the $200 million Georgia Aquarium and gave it debt free to the State of Georgia.

We are social beings and the human psyche is complex, but you can learn what works and what does not. Success is really living the life you want to lead, so why not begin on a path toward your own success.

Idea

The first step in becoming an entrepreneur is to be one. To think of how am I going to accumulate wealth? You can't make money but you can generate it. I have sold all type of things, hustled, and am always trying to think of money generating projects. Many individuals live in a scarcity mindset. They hold on to what they got, instead of increasing their pile and be in a winning position.

But it all starts with an idea. We all have skills and expertise. What are yours? Is there a need, a niche, something that you can provide quicker, better, and with a smile? In this shared economy it does not take much, simply hook onto the internet and bring a willing buyer and seller at the same time. Henry Ford shared that "Thinking is the hardest work there is, which is probably why so few engage in it." I am intellectual and my job is to think for a living.

So often we get caught up in the fog of war and lose sight of victory. As Arianna Huffington shares in her book *Thrive*, the key components of the new economy are creating a life of well-being, wisdom, and wonder. She also noted in a 2014 talk in Atlanta at SCAD that it is that third roommate in our head that keeps us from living our dreams. It says, we are too old, too dumb, too fat, or what other malarkey that it repeats. We fail to realize that we control that roommate. Check him out and check in a new one that is a cheerleader.

I can't tell you what business will guarantee your success. You probably will fail a few times. But remember that a JOB means **J**ust **O**ver **B**roke. There is no guarantee in the work place. There are no promises from your employer. One day you come in and your key card may not work and it's over. The shirking middle class is proof that they have lost in globalization expansion but never has it been easier for an entrepreneur to join in the game.

Initiative

This biggest challenge in any venture is to have a vision and an initiative of what you want to do. A plan. Do you want a better financial life? Do you want to find a solution to a problem in our world? Do you want to leave an imprint? It starts with a vision. A dream. Seems like children have no problem having a dream. They see the world around them full of wonder. They are in discovery mode and everything is an adventure. Children have a vast imagination and have not been locked into a mental track.

We all need a plan. Where do you want to go? How do you want to change the world? How do you want to create a business or find a solution to the world's problems? There are endless methods to develop a plan. It is a good exercise because it forces you to take on that dream and develop action steps. A dream is a dream unless you act on it. For the few that are big dreamers and spirit have not been crushed, you need to take action. Tom Peters writes about living in the WOW. Having a perspective to be in a World of Wonder. To have a constant lens of opportunity.

Life is more than simply working 30 years and retiring, it is a series of passages and adventures. The entrepreneur spirit makes it more of an adventure. There are lots of books out there on developing a business plan, so I won't go into the nitty gritty here, but I want to emphasize that you need to write it out. To have it down on paper and look at it. To focus. Now that you have a plan, you need to execute it and be willing to change and adapt. Be ready when you are punched in the face and adapt and execute. Move forward.

Where do you want to go? We are often afraid of money, of wealth. Of having economic security. Zig Ziglar would say money is not everything, there are stocks, bonds, and property. Seriously, we need to forget about the money. It will come. We got to center our attentions on passion. You don't make money, only the Federal Reserve does. If you do make money, you will go to jail for counterfeit. Money is faith in our system, faith in America, faith in "we the people".

Jim Clifton, CEO of the Gallup organization spoke to this at the HOPE conference in January 2015 in Atlanta. He surveyed 150 countries to understand what people desired.

The question was "What do you want more than anything else in the word?" He expected some utopian dreams, like peace in the world, love, harmony, better environment. The number one thing that came back was a "good job". He chronicles these findings in detail the challenges in his book *The Job Wars*.

As an entrepreneur you need to create a plan, to have a vision and then have steps to implement that plan. Start off with a piece of paper, spell out what it is you want to do. What is your business, how much money you need. It amazes me how many people approach me and tell me they are entrepreneurs but don't have a plan, or the type of business or don't know how much capital they need.

Yes, inspiration strikes, but you need a plan of attack. What often happens is that we get inspired and that euphoria stops when we hit obstacles and lose sight of what is it we want. A written down plan helps you to focus and is a step to making your vision a reality.

My dissertation was on organizations and measuring change with the component of leadership, culture, and public policy. I examined the most successful and controversial public institution, the Social Security Administration. Before I focused on that topic which is a whole other book, I was curious and am still fascinated in economic development. How some communities blossomed and other crumbled? What are the tenet that create a haven for entrepreneurs?

With social media and the interconnectedness of the internet you can find a niche and succeed in it. With 7 billion people on the planet, it has never been easier to go direct to consumer. All you need is one good ideal to blow up and scale fast.

You got to be ready for that defining moment. The second someone comes in and says I want to invest a million dollars into your business. You got to be ready for that moment that you are waiting for.

Internal Drive

Internal Drive is really the key component that separates the winners from the losers. To do whatever it takes. You see individuals that rise to the top. Many of the overnight successes have been working on their dreams for thirty years. My drive to be a speaker began when I was fourteen and spoke to middle school kids. I knew I had a gift. I needed ideas behind my words and I went on a quest for knowledge. I work on my craft every day and listen to good speakers and pull from my experiences. So I am always seeking new adventures. I wake up early, show up and take notes. That's way I have read over 10,000 books in the last decade.

What happens is that we don't feel like it. I am going do it later. A whole litany of excuses. That is the biggest reason for failure, you never actually tried.

Robert Schuller was fond of saying what would you do if you knew you would not fail? Well, duh, you would do it. But many of us allow that third roommate in our head talks us out of an opportunity. No, we are not smart enough, not good looking enough, too old, too young, an immigrant, a redneck, on and on, "stinking thinking" is easy to fall for. But if you do fail, then show up, stand up, and stand out again and again. To be a successful entrepreneur you need a vision, a plan, and do whatever it takes.

Never has it been so easy to create a business, to find a solution, to connect with people around the planet, so why not do it. I'll tell you why. It's hard, it's dirty, and it's scary. But in the end, why not do it. Why not be an entrepreneur and be part of a revolution. Be in the driver seat.

Island

Ok, with an idea, initiative, and the internal drive in place you got to simply "do it" and find an island where this idea will take off. The free market is tough and you can have everything in place but it does not take off. Be flexible and don't be afraid to ask and replicate what others are doing. Luck is when opportunity and preparedness come together, be ready to test your luck. Find that slice of where you have a change to succeed and beat the competition.

Don't reinvent the wheel, just make it better. It is ok if you don't want to be an entrepreneur, you can work 20 or 30 years and hope that the pension and Social Security will be there for you. But for those who dream big, take a chance.

To keep up with the opportunities of the time. One example is how live streaming and social media is changing business but it also is opening access. Now you can compete with the fortune 500 and 100 companies. Be quick and adapt to new silos of opportunity.

The newest kid on the social media block is the ease of live streaming. Periscope lead the way and as rank as the best app of 2015 The numbers speak for themselves. If you are one of the users or viewers of live streaming you are considered an early adopter. Only 2% of the 300 million Twitter users are active on periscope. That is downloaded the app, broadcasters are even fewer. Others exist, Meerkat, blab, and Facebook even has a feature.

We tend to forget that more people don't know us than do. This is why Coca-Cola works on domination of the soda market. Only a billion people on the planet drink a coke a day and with 7 billion on the planet, they have room for market growth.

There are many type of entrepreneurs, they can be for profit entrepreneurs, social entrepreneurs, but they have three common ingredients. They have a vision, a plan, and do whatever it takes.

But how do you develop a vision? You need to sit and reflect. Slow down and listen to the voice inside. What are your passions? What do you love to do? Take assessment and ask, "How did I get here?" What were the decisions that brought me here? Some have had a direct path, but most don't. Most have been muddling through approach. We float along and then realize one day that life is over.

I read years ago that most individuals have seven major decisions that shape their destiny. The choices maybe as simple as where we live or how we deal with death in our lives. Who we marry or live with, where we decide to call home. Life is a series of "T"s, like a train track, we can go left or right. Both are full of different set of circumstances. We can analyze our situations and find out how we got here, but more importantly can we predict where we are going?

The only certainty of our future is that we are going to die. That we have a limited amount of time, mortality has a way to really force you to wake up. Steve Jobs shared in his commencement speeches these quotes:

"Remember that you are going to die is the best way I know to avoid the trap of thinking you have something to lose."

"Your time is limited, so why waste it living someone else's life"

"History rarely yields to one person, but think and never forget, what happens when it does. That can be you. That should be you. That must be you."

"All these center on our limited time on this spinning ball

of mud, earth. Why not take risks and be entrepreneurial?"

"This will make you wake up and realize that you can take charge and create a path for your life."

"To develop a mission. Sit down and write down what you want to accomplish and start doing it."

Entrepreneurship helps you be innovative and find a method to accomplishing this vision. In business, it is important for organization to remind themselves, what do I do and why do I do it? Often it is the losing focus that ends a business. Or not accessing the world around and be willing to change.

Innovate

At the Atlanta 2015 Social Shake up conference Mark Hatch, CEO of Techshop shared the successful creation of innovation centers in communities in the San Francisco Bay area. With an average of a $4 million dollar investment, these centers provide a foundation for idea makers, entrepreneurs, and any one with inspiration to have access to the latest technologies. Be it 3D printers, manufactural cutters, or top computer power, the concept is easy, anyone can have access if they pay a minimal membership fee.

These centers are more than just business, they create a platforms for community. They have classes, sponsor cool events like laser cutting "date" nights and provide economic centers for areas that have been blighted.

So far, these "innovation centers" have created jobs, new businesses, and new products. The world's fastest electric motorcycle was created there. We have all seen those small square devices that attach to the iPhone where independent merchants can swipe credit cards came from there.

So much is written about the slow moving economic

engine in the United States but we fail to remind ourselves of the American innovative spirit. Three of the top world companies came from the USA: Apple, Google, and Microsoft. Amazon value has surpassed Wal-Mart and the valuation increase was their expansion into marketing cloud space.

The innovation spirit is ingrained in the US DNA, but it is key to note what makes these innovators shine. We must wake America from its funk and say '"hey we can do it". Let's create a new world full of economic opportunity.

As Walter Isaacson writes in his book *The Innovators*, he notes that individuals that have changed the paradigm were able to merge science and creativity. In this interconnected age we can leverage social media with what futurist Jim Carrol says is the ability to "think big, start small and scale fast". The scaling has accelerated the tipping point.

When we observe individual innovators, Malcom Gladwell shares that one aspect is that they are "different" and really don't care what others think of them. These "innovators" are able to see a problem differently, tackle it head first, and discover a not traditional solution. They solve a challenge or fulfill a need.

We are a nation of immigrants and each of us are unique. Instead of the European model of "maintaining the culture" and being afraid of change, the US has always thrived on it. Our "can do" attitude has pushed the boundaries of the imagination and led us to all the way up to the moon and back. America has the synergy to foster those who want to seek a path. We have forgotten that we are in the land of opportunity. Every dramatic shift of human civilization came from the collapse of an existing world order. We are experiencing that entrance into the blossoming of the information age.

So now the next time you see someone that is different from you, celebrate that uniqueness. Celebrate your own individual traits and don't be afraid to break from the pack. Who knows, that quality may change the world as we know it. Think like a superhero. The superhero stands up for his ideals. Has vision. Use these superpowers to solve a problem and always be aware of the world around. What is your super powers? What can you do better than anyone else? On the reverse, what is your kryptonite? What are your weaknesses? Don't dwell on these but seek others that thrive. Can you fill the gap? Seek a team of excellence.

American needs to gets its "groove" back and support entrepreneurs and change agents. By taking the steps of entrepreneurship of the five Is: Idea, initiative, internal drive, island, and innovate, you have a road map to create the next big thing. Small business and entrepreneurs have always run the economy. Move to the next level and become an entrepreneur and help American become great again.

> "All great changes are preceded by chaos."
> Deepak Chopra

Chapter 4 Action

"If it's going to be, it's up to me!"
Robert H. Schuller

Talk is cheap. Unless you take assessment into your own life and organization and do something, nothing will happen. Action is the key to success.

We live in the golden age of civilization and have more opportunity available to us than ever. Information is everywhere, the challenge is to access what is relevant to you. To take action. Decide. Look at our political system. The pressing problems of today exist because our leaders have opted to "kick the can down the road" rather than stand up and fight. To make hard choices that will secure a better tomorrow. The same with many individuals. They fail to take action and do something. All they do is whine about it. You got to take responsibility for all the good and bad decision in your life, instead of being the victim. It is easy to complain, it is hard to stand up and fight. You need to show up, stand up, and stand out.

I need you to fight. To awaken those long lost dreams and decide that you will do whatever it takes. The only moment we have is this second. This opportunity that you and I engage. The past is gone and the future is not a guarantee, we exist in the now. In other words the past is a ghost, the future is dream, all we have is today.

The Dalai Lama says we have three things that

bring us together, we all have mamas, we all want to be happy, and we are all going to die, not if but when. I heard Warren Buffet share at a 2015 Coca Cola stockholder's meeting that he would trade all his money and fame from his 84 years to be a child born in the USA today. He realizes the awesome opportunity. Why don't you?

Studies in human psychology show that we learn best by modeling. We become the parents we had, we are the friends we have experienced, we become the bosses we have known.

Malcolm Gladwell in his writings has popularized the 10,000 hour rule. This means that if you want to be a genius or expert you need to put in 10,000 hours. Seems a lot, but not really, it is what it takes to get whatever information or skill to become second nature to you. I have read more books that I can remember but in the last 4 years I have read over 1,700 books. This has made me realize the more I learn, the less I know. But it also has added to my broad base of knowledge. An education does that. A formula, a path that will help you curve the 10,000 hours.

What I have done, is create a path, a formula, a mantra for my own journey. After studying leaders and success, I wanted a simple template. This is what I call my ABCs. They stand for my Attitude, Beliefs, and Commitment. Then have a vision to follow through. The ABC Vision template stands for ideas and reaching success.

According to Earl Nightingale, "success is the progressive realization of a worthy ideal". Success goes to the businessman who wants to provide a service or product. Success goes to the school teacher who wants to touch the future by teaching. Success goes to the policeman who wants to make our cities safe. We all have our own vision of who we are. The challenge is to become the person we want to be and transform that vision of ourselves into who we are.

All great structures have a good foundation and the ABCs are a template to help us constantly get realign with our plan. To go in the direction that will enable us to move up the ladder of success.

One best way to observe what it takes is to look at how children interact. When you see young children in grade school, regardless of race, color, or gender, you see them full of hope and optimism. They have a core sense of self and do not get caught up in the limitations imposed by society. They are excited about life, eager to learn, and are not afraid to challenge conventional wisdom. Together, they play and explore their world with a sense of excitement. Like sponges, they soak up ideas and live life. Ask them what they want to do when they are grownups and they will give you a list of exciting occupations, such as astronauts, firemen, and doctors.

Now fast forward to what is commonly found with adults. They become zombies. Visit a local government office or large corporation. The place has the energy zapped and you can sense the lack of enthusiasm, hope, and optimism. It is as though the spirit has been drained out of them. They have traded their dreams for a paycheck and a retirement plan. These folks just exist, they don't live. We have known people who can't get out of bed because they hate what they do and feel trapped in their bleak world. How can we have forgotten what we took for granted in childhood? Children love, dream and play.

They celebrate adventure and creativity.

One reason for this complacency is that we have so many blessings in our world. Never before has it been easier to make a living, never before has it been so easy to blend into the background and disconnect from society. These are many good things, but also bad things, never before have people been so lonely. They are drowning in information and starving from attention.

But to get the love, you got to give the love. To find opportunity, you need to seek it. Ask and you shall receive. I wrote a book on love that expands on this message of intention.

Life is not a destination but a journey filled with experiences and lessons. The purpose of life is a life of purpose. Our purpose and what makes us happy is to help others. That is why I am called to public service and to speak to audiences across the world. I believe that service is the price you pay for living. To share ideas and spread the message of peace, love, and opportunity.

The wisdom in this book is useless unless you are willing to take action. The best time to act is today, so start anew, time is ticking away. As Ben Franklin was fond of saying, "Lost time is never found again." So don't count the days, but make the days count. Keep reminding yourself that life begins now. Dare to soar and live with passion.

Attitude = Vision = Where do you want to go?

Writer and philosopher Wayne Dyer shares that "attitude is everything, so pick one." Abraham Lincoln once said, "we're just about as happy as we make our minds to be" and how true it is.

Every day you face new challenges and obstacles. The only way you can overcome this is to determine the attitude you will have. This means that what you feed your mind determines the person you become. So simple. Yes. Think of this as a simple equation- negative in equals negative out, positive in equals positive out. You, and you alone, can control what your mind accepts or rejects. Good attitudes are contagious, is yours worth catching?

Inside our own heads we have competing forces, but we can set the tone to which one dictates our state. We have many, but the dominate ones are joy, fear, disgust, and safety. But some reactions we can't control, like learning of the death of a love one. Or when our heart is broken into a million pieces by rejection.

Life is not your enemy, but your thinking can be. By controlling your thoughts you can control your outcome. Accept responsibility for your present state. It will free you from blaming others for the situation that you find yourself in.

Learn to let go of the past. Deepak Chopra says holding on to the past is like holding on to a breath. Try to hold your breath, do it now, hold it… hold it… hold it. Don't let go. Now let go, what did you discover. If you hold your breath you will suffocate.

Now that you have taken responsibility, make an honest assessment of your life and pinpoint where you stand. Review what you are grateful for and what is in your control that can or will make you happy. We can't change the past. But we can reboot and change the present, to begin on a new path. Death is the only obstacle we cannot overcome.

What are your dreams? Take action in seeking a means of attaining what you want. Create a vision of where you want to go. Concentrate on listening to the inner voice of truth and it will never lead you astray. Go ahead, write your dreams down. These are goals.

Beliefs = Core Values = Why do I want to do this?

Take the first step and become determined to live the dreams and seek the inner power to do so. Your beliefs are the core of your being. They determine your actions and reactions. Believe in yourself and remember that you are an original. You are in control. No one can make you feel inferior unless you let them do so. Break free from the limitations of the past. Don't ever underestimate your power to make a difference. Climb to new heights and discover the awesome view!

Write out your mission statement, list your goals, and remind yourself that you have a reason for believing.

Steven Covey in his *Seven Habits of Highly Effective People* goes deep into the question of beliefs. To understand why you do the things you do. Successful people have an end purpose. They fight for what they believe in and take on the challenges that may come on the way to accomplishing their goals. This is a continuous process. Reach one mountain, conquer it and move on to another. We change and so should our goals.

Commitment = Focus = How will I get there?

Choose to live life today. Your commitment is your focus and will determine how you will get to your destination. How do cut down an oak tree? You don't cut it down but sawing right through the trunk, but by cutting one branch at a time. That makes it manageable and systematically possible to cart the tree away. This simple principle also applies to your life; one step at a time moves you toward your destination.

Change is inevitable. Accept continual change and change before you have to. No one can change until they really want to change. Covey speaks to the key of life, "Between stimulus and response, there is a space. In that space, lies our freedom and power to choose our response. In those choices will lay our growth and happiness".

Create a clear vision. You can have the life you want, but you have to know your destination in advance and desire it with all your heart. Write down your goals and outline the steps needed to reach them. Without a definite goal and a plan of action to achieve it, you cannot reach your destination. Be committed to change and handle the daily challenges of life. Realize that if it's going to be, it's up to me. You are the only one who can determine the outcome of your personal story. Think of the laws of the harvest: farmers do not procrastinate; they must get out and plant the seeds, work the land, and reap the benefits of their labor. In life, as in farming, you cannot cram the night before and expect to reap a good harvest. How can you enjoy your goals of tomorrow, if you don't work toward them today? Know where you are going and focus on the finish line. Be committed to your goals, for without discipline, you can do nothing in this world, nothing! No matter what happens, always, always remember that the past is fact, the present is reality, and the future is possibility. Continue the journey by moving forward.

We are born alone and die alone, but the journey is filled with relationships. These connections are what help us either rise up or sink. Why not seek to rise up? Social media is really a cloning of our collective soul. We can now with a press of a button seek out all the resources the world has to offer. We can share our thoughts, spread "aha" moments, or simply vent. We can build our fan base. Our cheerleaders.

Our emotions come into play in our decisions. We tend to buy those product or services from people we like. We determine value from what we get. Life is really a series of moments, of things that impact us. We carry these memories with us. Social media allows us to share our story, our journey, our own perspective. Stories are really memories, tales that capture our legacy.

The most intimate way you can connect with someone is to read their words. To get inside their heads. I am sitting in my study as I write this, I am processing my years of experience into this book. Trying to lay out my methods and reach out and share with you so that you can take some of these gems and apply them to your life. Unlike previous writing projects, I am not using a typewriter or laptop. I am using my smart tablet, an iPad to churn out this book.

The vision is yours. Our manifest destiny can be created. Business, personal, and society all interconnect. The foundation is you. What do you do, how do you do it, and how are you going to measure it? Money is not everything but it represents faith, freedom, and power. Don't be afraid to get paid what you are worth and share the blessings.

Love is the answer. Use that emotional intelligence of yours and be curious and be willing to open yourself up to love your fellow seven billion compadres on this planet.

I read an interview in *Time* magazine where Astronaut Terry Virts recalled a story by a friend, a fellow astronaut, Mike Fincke was asked before the space launch about his favorite planet. "Is it Mars? Is it Jupiter?" He simply responded 'My favorite planet is Earth.'" Yes, the blue marble is an oasis in the universe, remember how special you are to be living in this golden age of civilization on this blue marble. We are one verse, the universe.

Dr. Wilson Lubin Triviño @abcvision

"The only place where your dreams become impossible is in your own thinking"
Robert H. Schuller

Chapter 5 Dream Big

"You don't win if you don't begin!!!"
Robert H. Schuller

All the great companies and accomplishments have one thing in common. They started inside someone's head. It was an idea, it was a dream, it was an inspiration. You don't have to be struck by lightning or banged across the head for something to come into your mind. You just have to think. To believe. To take time and reflect on solutions to the world's problems. IBM's founder Thomas J. Watson focus was on one word, "Think". He posted it everywhere.

We have forgotten in our hyper connected fast pace world to think. To use that brain and intellectual power that all of us possess. You don't have to be book smart or have a wall full of degrees to create. You just need a will to do so. A willingness to put in your two cents. Our brains react to what we put in it. Put fear and fear comes out, put greatness and greatness comes out, mix in some love and love comes out. You get the message.

The building where my office is located is the Innovation Center. The reason it is called that is that it is a spot where ideas are created. Where dreams become reality. The awesome power of ideas is that unlike money or tangible things, everyone benefits. If I have a penny and you have a penny, and I give you a penny then you have two pennies and I have none. If I have an idea and you have an idea then I give you an idea then we both come away with two ideas. This is true power.

Studies have show we have over 50,000-70,000 thoughts pass through our mind a day. It breaks down to 35 and 48 per minute per person. Surely one of those has the power to change the course of our lives. Change the course of civilization! But what happens is we allow stinky thinking to invade our minds. The naysayers, the ones that that tell us it cannot happen. The ones that are road blocks to our evolution. The road blocks that come up and stop us cold in our tracks.

We are bombarded by information and stimulation all the time. We forget that we are in control, we can control what comes in and what goes in. You need to calm the mind and relish the quiet. To be able to focus on what is important and what is fluff. The power of the mind is great. Look at all the wonderful things great minds have created. Technology, modern civilization, and our way of life. We have something today that is more important than anything else. It is the power to control our thoughts. The ability to see something and make it come true. No matter how outrageous, as long as we are committed to our dreams, nothing can stop us. What happens is we allow life's road blocks to stumble our progress.

Take a moment and think what you would do if you could not fail? What would you tackle? What you would do. Some call it a bucket list, but I call it a dream list. That vision that comes to us, but we fail to take hold and grab. You may say that sounds too easy, but it is. It is as easy as seeing it and creating a path to get it.

Deepak Chopra calls it the "spontaneous fulfillment

of desire", have you ever had a thought a dream or intuition and it comes to be. All of a sudden doors open and opportunities present themselves that never happen before? This is what Dr. Schuller called "possibility thinking". To make the impossible possible. Schuller shared a story how hope is the ability to move into the tomorrow. To break through and initiate a new path. A way to overcome the stagnation we see. Frank Sinatra told him once that "Dr. Schuller, your messages are medicine to my mind. Somehow, every time I listen, I have the courage to step into tomorrow." Wow, the courage to step into tomorrow. That's is really what we can hope for. You can step into the future you are given or create the future you want.

Today we live in a world full of bad noise. Of despair, but we forget as Dr. Schuller stated, "Tough times never last, but tough people do." It is the that window of opportunity we must open. Life is not a direct line of progression, it is a full of hills and valleys, a few mountains along the way. It is up to us to climb those mountains. To decide to take on the adventure of our life time and opt to live on the sunny side of the mountain rather than in the shadow. It is easy to cave into fear. But it is up to us to stand up. Zig Ziglar called FEAR as the false evidence that appears real. It is that false perception that triggers the stagnant emotions that will stop our progression.

You might say, how do I dream big? Well, imagine if you could do anything and not fail? How awesome would that be? Sound trivial, absurd, silly? Yes, but what other option do you have? Not do anything? That is the easy route, to allow these problems to become road blocks instead of a fast land to success.

Dream big, grab a pen and start writing. What do I want to do if I knew I could not fail. Without thinking, just write here what comes out. Go big, be bold and celebrate this day.

DREAM BIG-

----WRITE THEM DOWN HERE----

Chapter 6 Get Up & Ignite the Hustle

"Tough times never last but tough people do."
Robert Schuller

Here we are, back in my bed at 4 am on Christmas Eve, listening to Rockabilly music and humming along my favorite Brian Setzer tunes. Trying to keep my pencil up to speed as my brain races with ideas.

As a Christian, tonight is the night. The day Christ was born. How he and his ideas changed the world. But his message is timeless regardless of your faith. To love your neighbor like yourself, forgive, and no matter what happens, it will all work out. Life is not that complicated, but we make it so. This journey is so fast that we need to celebrate every moment. One day it will be over. We will transition to what ever the next big thing is going to be.

You are destine to greatness. You just have to figure out what you want that to be.

One reason why I love Rockabilly is comes from a short period in the late 50s where the sound was a transition from the crooner big band music into Rock 'n Roll. The mix of hillbilly, blues, and rock hits a twang that reflects the rebel feel. I know I am a rebel, ready to challenge the status quo. To break things down and make them better. These rockabilly guys and gals were trail blazers and pushed us into the age of space travel and the digital information age.

We are blessed to live in this golden age of civilization. As Peggy Noonan's memoir *In Our Time* points to, we need to live in our time. The buzz of politics, economics, pop culture are all part of what makes our world exciting. We can't shut one part out. We need to embrace the shift and change. The world is in transition. We can't hold back, we need to move forward. This book is a catalyst for this change.

We need to accept that there is a lot of fear and trouble in the world. As Billy Joel's song says "I did not start the fire" but I can help extinguish it. I don't understand the mind of the terrorist to create chaos. But I will not live in fear.

We must have the commitment to success as he pig in breakfast. Where the chicken is present in the eggs, the pig is committed in the bacon. Every day you need to focus on your commitment. LEAD is a template to refocus on being great.

L- Leadership

Become a leader. Set an example, realize that you can be the person you want to be. Thousands of books have been written. Lessons from others lives. Seek out a path and learn from others. That is why ideas are so valuable. Develop that leader within you.

E- Entrepreneurship

Use the mind of the entrepreneur to face you daily challenges to solve problems. Seek solutions and develop a framework of exceptionalism. Entrepreneurs exist in the private and public sector.

A- Actions

Take proactive steps to live your dreams. Create a plan, implement it. How many of us have the same goals everyday. But never reach them. We fail to take action.

D- Dream Big

Be outrageous! If you are lucky you live to be 80, 90,

or 100 years old. Why not go all out. See yourself beyond yourself. Be a no limit person.

Break free from your worse critic- YOU. Say I cannot I can't.

Believe in you. I do. If I did not I would not have written this book. There are lots of other books out there. But I think this one is different. Direct and to the point.

Finally, ignite the hustle. A spark to start that fire. Burn that blaze and heat up that desire. Tony Robbins shares that "the past does not equal the future" so begin a new future today. Start a new journey. Be grateful, be humble, and leave this journey without any regret. Life is short, be awesome and I hope to see you soon.

As my vintage 1980 Ronald Reagan poster say on wall of my office at the innovation center states "Let's Make America great again."

Yes! Together we can succeed.

"You never suffer from a money problem, you always suffer from an idea problem"
Robert H. Schuller

References

Brinkley, Douglas. 2004. Wheels for the World: Henry Ford, His Company, and a Century of Progress. New York City: NY. Penguin Books.

Bryant, John Hope. 2014. How the Poor Can Save Capitalism: Rebuilding the Path to the Middle Class. New York City, NY: Berrett-Koeler Publishers.

Cardone, Grant. 2010. If You're Not First, You're Last: Sales Strategies to Dominate Your Market and Beat Your Competition. New York City, NY: Wiley.

Carnegie, Dale. 1984. How to Stop Worrying and Start Living. New York, NY: Simon and Schuster.

Ciandella, Don. March 29, 1984. *Space Kid: Wilson Trivino's 'A Walking Encyclopedia'*. Marietta Daily Journal. B1.

Chopra, Deepak. 2004. The Spontaneous Fulfillment of Desire: Harnessing the Infinite Power of Coincidence. New York City, NY: Harmony.

Clifton, Jim. 2011. The Coming Wars. New York City: NY: Gallup Press.

Collins, Jim and Morten Hansen. 2011. Great by Choice. New York, NY: Harper Collins, Inc.

Coupland, Douglas. 1991. Generation X: Tales for an Accelerated Culture. New York City, NY: St. Martin's Griffin.

Covey, Stephen R. 1990. The 7 Habits of Highly Effective People. New York, NY: Simon & Schuster, Inc.

Dyer, Wayne W. 1989. You've Seen it When You Believe it. New York, NY: Avon Books.

Dyer, Wayne W. 1992. Real Magic: Creating Miracles in Everyday Life. New York, NY: Harper Books.

Dyer, Wayne W. 1998. Wisdom of the Ages. New York, NY: Harper Collins Books.

Friedman, Thomas. 2005. The World is Flat: A Brief History of the Twenty-first Century. New York City, NY: Farrar, Straus, and Giroux.

Gladwell, Malcolm. 2002. The Tipping Point: How Little Things Can Make a Big Difference. New York City, NY: Back Bay Books.

Hackett, Pat. Edited. 1989. The Andy Warhol Diaries. New York City, NY: Warner Books.

Huffington, Arianna. 2014. Thrive: The Third Metrix to Redefining Success and Creating a life of Well-being, Wisdom, and Wonder. New York City, NY: Harmony.

Isaac, Mike and Vindu Goel. March 26, 2015. *As Twitter Introduces Periscope, Tech Titans Bet on Live Streaming Videos.* New York Times. IA.

Isaacson, Walter. 2014. The Innovators: How a Group of Hackers, Geniuses, and Geeks Created the Digital Revolution. New York City, NY: Simon and Schuster.

Katz, Andrew. June 23, 2015. "Exclusive: Astronaut Terry Virtz on the Power of Space Photography. Online Time.

Lama, Dalai and Howard Cutler, MD. 2009. The Art of Happiness in a Troubled World. New York City, NY: Harmony.

Littell, Robert S. 2001. Power Netweaving: 10 Secrets to Successful Relationship Marketing. New York City, NY: National Underwriter Company.

Mackay, Harvey. 1990. Dig Your Well Before You're Thirsty. New York, NY: Batman Doubleday Publishing Group.

Noonan, Peggy. 2015. The Time of Our Lives: Collected Writings. New York, NY: Twelve.

Peale, Norman Vincent. 1952. The Power of Positive Thinking and the Amazing Results of Positive Thinking. New York, NY: Prentice-Hall.

Peters, Tom and Robert H. Waterman. 1982. In Search of Excellence. New York, NY: Harper & Row.

Putnam, Robert. 2001. Bowling Alone: The Collaspse and Revival of American Community. New York City, NY: Touchstone.

Reiman, Joey. 1998. Thinking for A Living. Marietta, GA: Longstreet.

Rusk, Sebastian. 2014. Social Media Sucks: (If You Don't Know What You're Doing). Charleston, South Carolina: Advantage.

Sandburg, Carl. 1991. Remembrance Rock. New York City, NY: Mariner Books.

Schuller, Robert H. 1983. Tough Times Never Last But Tough People Do! Nashville, Tennesee: Thomas Nelson.

Schuller, Robert H. 1986. You Can Become the Person You want to Be. New York City, NY: Jove.

Schuller, Robert H. 1987. The Be (Happy) Attitudes. Irving, TX: Batman Books.

Schuller, Robert H. 1991. Power Thoughts: Achieve Your True Potential Through Thinking. New York, NY: Harper Paper Back Books.

Triviño, Wilson. 2003. Remember Your ABCs: A Simple Guide on how to become a Success and live the life YOU want to lead!. Marietta, GA: Aura Free Press.

Triviño, Wilson. 2015. ABCs of Live Streaming: Harness the Power of Live Streaming. Marietta, GA: Aura Free Press.

Vaynerchuk, Gary. 2013. Jab, Jab, Jab, Right Hook: How to Tell Your Story in a Noisy Social World. New York: NY: Harper Business.

White, Theodore H. 2009. The Making of the President 1960. New York. Harper Perennial Political Classics.

Ziglar, Zig. 1994. <u>Over the Top: Moving from Survival to Stability, from Stability to Success To Significance</u>. Nashville, TN: Thomas Nelson, Inc.

Ziglar, Zig. 1999. <u>Something Else to Smile About</u>. Nashville, TN: Thomas Nelson, Inc.

"One"
C. David Triviño, Esq.

About the Author

Political Scientist Dr. Wilson L. Triviño is a writer, thinker, and lover.

Triviño was the first Latino to receive a doctorate in Public Policy and Public Administration from Auburn University in Auburn, Alabama. He holds a Masters in Public Administration from Auburn University and a Bachelor of Arts from Kennesaw State University.

If you would like to interview Dr. Wilson L. Triviño, book to speak at your next event; review a product or a cool social occasion, contact him at Twitter / Instagram / Snaptchat / @abcvision or abcvision@hotmail.com

Check out his live stream show on Periscope @abcvision

Buy his six other books on Amazon

Read his column at www.purepolitics.com

He resides in Atlanta, Georgia USA.